4/26/03

David Farragut

Union Admiral

To the students of SJB,

keep reading!

Best wishes,

[signature]

Colonial Leaders

Lord Baltimore
English Politician and Colonist

Benjamin Banneker
American Mathematician and Astronomer

Sir William Berkeley
Governor of Virginia

William Bradford
Governor of Plymouth Colony

Jonathan Edwards
Colonial Religious Leader

Benjamin Franklin
American Statesman, Scientist, and Writer

Anne Hutchinson
Religious Leader

Cotton Mather
Author, Clergyman, and Scholar

Increase Mather
Clergyman and Scholar

James Oglethorpe
Humanitarian and Soldier

William Penn
Founder of Democracy

Sir Walter Raleigh
English Explorer and Author

Caesar Rodney
American Patriot

John Smith
English Explorer and Colonist

Miles Standish
Plymouth Colony Leader

Peter Stuyvesant
Dutch Military Leader

George Whitefield
Clergyman and Scholar

Roger Williams
Founder of Rhode Island

John Winthrop
Politician and Statesman

John Peter Zenger
Free Press Advocate

Revolutionary War Leaders

John Adams
Second U.S. President

Samuel Adams
Patriot

Ethan Allen
Revolutionary Hero

Benedict Arnold
Traitor to the Cause

John Burgoyne
British General

George Rogers Clark
American General

Lord Cornwallis
British General

Thomas Gage
British General

King George III
English Monarch

Nathanael Greene
Military Leader

Nathan Hale
Revolutionary Hero

Alexander Hamilton
First U.S. Secretary of the Treasury

John Hancock
President of the Continental Congress

Patrick Henry
American Statesman and Speaker

William Howe
British General

John Jay
First Chief Justice of the Supreme Court

Thomas Jefferson
Author of the Declaration of Independence

John Paul Jones
Father of the U.S. Navy

Thaddeus Kosciuszko
Polish General and Patriot

Lafayette
French Freedom Fighter

James Madison
Father of the Constitution

Francis Marion
The Swamp Fox

James Monroe
American Statesman

Thomas Paine
Political Writer

Molly Pitcher
Heroine

Paul Revere
American Patriot

Betsy Ross
American Patriot

Baron Von Steuben
American General

George Washington
First U.S. President

Anthony Wayne
American General

Famous Figures of the Civil War Era

John Brown
Abolitionist

Jefferson Davis
Confederate President

Frederick Douglass
Abolitionist and Author

Stephen A. Douglas
Champion of the Union

David Farragut
Union Admiral

Ulysses S. Grant
Military Leader and President

Stonewall Jackson
Confederate General

Joseph E. Johnston
Confederate General

Robert E. Lee
Confederate General

Abraham Lincoln
Civil War President

George Gordon Meade
Union General

George McClellan
Union General

William Henry Seward
Senator and Statesman

Philip Sheridan
Union General

William Sherman
Union General

Edwin Stanton
Secretary of War

Harriet Beecher Stowe
Author of Uncle Tom's Cabin

James Ewell Brown Stuart
Confederate General

Sojourner Truth
Abolitionist, Suffragist, and Preacher

Harriet Tubman
Leader of the Underground Railroad

Famous Figures of the Civil War Era

David Farragut

Union Admiral

Bruce Adelson

Arthur M. Schlesinger, jr.
Senior Consulting Editor

Chelsea House Publishers

Philadelphia

CHELSEA HOUSE PUBLISHERS
Editor-in-Chief Sally Cheney
Director of Production Kim Shinners
Production Manager Pamela Loos
Art Director Sara Davis
Production Editor Diann Grasse

Staff for *DAVID FARRAGUT*
Editor Sally Cheney
Associate Art Director Takeshi Takahashi
Series Design Keith Trego
Layout by D&G Limited, LLC

The Chelsea House World Wide Web address is
http://www.chelseahouse.com

First Printing
1 3 5 7 9 8 6 4 2

Library of Congress Cataloging-in-Publication Data

Adelson, Bruce.
 David Farragut : Union Admiral / Bruce Adelson.
  p. cm. — (Famous figures of the Civil War era)
 Includes bibliographical references and index.
 ISBN 0-7910-6416-6 (alk. paper) — ISBN 0-7910-6417-4 (pbk. :
 alk. paper)
  1. Farragut, David Glasgow, 1801-1870—Juvenile literature.
 2. Admirals—United States—Biography—Juvenile literature.
 3. United States. Navy—Biography—Juvenile literature. 4. United
 States—History—Civil War, 1861-1865—Naval operations—
 Juvenile literature. 5. United States—History, Naval—To 1900—
 Juvenile literature. [1. Farragut, David Glasgow, 1801-1870.
 2. Admirals. 3. United States—History—Civil War, 1861-1865—
 Naval operations. 4. United States—History, Naval—To 1900.]
 I. Title. II. Series.

 E467.1.F23 A34 2001
 973.7'58—dc21

 2001028767

Publisher's Note: In Colonial, Revolutionary War, and Civil War Era America, there were no standard rules for spelling, punctuation, capitalization, or grammar. Some of the quotations that appear in the Colonial Leaders, Revolutionary War Leaders, and Famous Figures of the Civil War Era series come from original documents and letters written during this time in history. Original quotations reflect writing inconsistencies of the period.

Contents

1 Young Sailor 7

2 A Country Divided 23

3 The Hero of New Orleans 35

4 "Damn the Torpedoes!" 47

5 War Hero 63

Glossary 73

Chronology 74

Civil War Time Line 75

Further Reading 77

Index 78

David Farragut was 11 years old when he served in the United States Navy as a midshipman during the War of 1812. Here the British ship *Macedonian* and the American ship *United States* fight near the Madeira Islands during the war.

Young Sailor

1

David Farragut was one of America's greatest naval war heroes, winning victories for the Northern states during the Civil War. Although he became a hero as an adult, David's career in the navy began when he was not even 10 years old, just before the United States went to war with Great Britain in 1812.

David Farragut was born on July 5, 1801 in Campbell's Station, Tennessee, a small town near the city of Knoxville. David was not the name his parents gave him when he was born. Instead, his parents, George and Elizabeth Farragut, named their new son James Glasgow Farragut.

George was a ferryboat operator, so ships and sailing were part of the Farragut family tradition. A ferryboat is a ship that carries passengers. As a boat operator, George was in charge of his own ferryboat, and sailed it on Tennessee's rivers. In 1807 the U.S. Navy offered George a job in Louisiana as a sailing master. This was a better position than ferryboat operator so George moved his family to New Orleans, Louisiana, where he began his new career. Sailing masters are responsible for many different kinds of boats in a harbor, not just ferryboats.

While in Louisiana, the Farraguts met a family called the Porters. Elizabeth Farragut took care of David Porter, the grandfather of the Porter family, who was old and very sick. Elizabeth herself became ill while taking care of him, and she died of yellow fever in 1808. David Porter died shortly after Elizabeth.

The Porters never forgot Elizabeth's kindness. They were a famous family. David Porter, the son of the man who died, was a Commander

David Porter became David Farragut's guardian and started him on a career in the navy as a midshipman in 1810.

in the U.S. Navy and in charge of the U.S. Naval base in New Orleans, where George Farragut worked.

After Elizabeth's death, Commander Porter offered to help young James Glasgow Farragut with his education and future. George Farragut accepted David's kind offer. David became James's guardian and took him to Washington, D.C. James had never been to Washington and was very excited. He now wanted to be a sailor, like his new guardian.

In Washington, James met many famous people, like Paul Hamilton, the Secretary of the Navy. The Secretary of the Navy is the person in the government who is in charge of the U.S. Navy. James told Secretary Hamilton that he wanted to be in the navy. Secretary Hamilton promised James that he would be a sailor before his 10th birthday. On December 17, 1810, James became a midshipman, the lowest ranking officer at that time in the U.S. Navy. Midshipman Farragut was only nine and a half years old.

In 1811, David Porter, who was now a captain in the navy, took Midshipman Farragut with him on a warship, the USS (that means United

States Ship) *Essex*. This was Farragut's first trip to sea on a warship. While he was part of the crew of the *Essex*, the War of 1812 began between the United States and Great Britain.

The war started for many reasons. The United States was angry that British ships stopped American ships at sea where British sailors removed British citizens they found on board. They also took American sailors away and forced them to serve in the British navy. In 1807 a British ship even fired on an American warship, the USS *Chesapeake*.

Finally, many representatives in the U.S. Congress demanded that Britain stop removing people from American ships. Great Britain refused. On June 18, 1812, President James Monroe signed the Declaration of War, and the War of 1812 began. Many Americans were worried about fighting Great Britain only about 30 years after the United States had won its independence from this country in the American Revolution. There were many Americans who feared that if Great Britain won the War of 1812, America would again become a British colony.

After the war began, Midshipman Farragut stayed with Captain Porter on board the USS *Essex*. In July and August, the *Essex* won several sea battles with small enemy ships in the Atlantic Ocean, near the United States. In September the navy ordered the *Essex* and two other American warships to go on a mission to South America. There, they would locate and sink British ships and destroy a large British fishery near Brazil.

The three American warships sailed to South America. In March 1813 the *Essex* left the other two ships and sailed around the southern tip of South America, called Cape Horn, to the Pacific Ocean.

Midshipman Farragut, then about eleven and a half years old, and the rest of the *Essex* crew worked hard to keep the ship under control while strong, cold winds and stormy seas shook the *Essex*. The waves rocked the ship from side to side. On March 3, when seawater burst into

David had many duties when he was a midshipman. One job was to be a powder boy. A powder boy on the Union warship *New Hampshire* is shown here. It was his job to bring gunpowder charges to the crew.

one side of the *Essex,* the crew was worried the ship could sink.

The USS *Essex* was an ironclad American warship that was involved in many sea battles near Chile. Midshipman Farragut became the commander of the USS *Essex Junior,* which was originally a British battle ship that had been captured by the *Essex.*

Despite the bad weather, the *Essex* survived, and soon passed safely around Cape Horn. On March 11 the warship arrived at the city of Valparaiso, Chile. At that time, Chile was part of Spain, which was an ally, or friend, of Great Britain and enemy of the United States.

The *Essex* was soon involved in many sea battles near Chile, capturing several enemy ships. In June 1813, when Midshipman Farragut was almost 12 years old, David Porter gave him command of his first ship, the *Alexander Barclay*, which had been captured by the *Essex*. It was unusual for someone so young to command a warship, but Captain Porter believed Midshipman Farragut would do a good job.

Captain Porter gave the *Alexander Barclay* a new name, the USS *Essex Junior*, named after the warship they had sailed on to South America. Midshipman Farragut was proud of his first command. Captain Porter watched how Farragut performed in his new job and was pleased with his performance.

For the rest of 1813, the *Essex* and *Essex Junior* captured other enemy **vessels.** The British were worried about these American warships. Two British warships, more powerful than the *Essex* and *Essex Junior*, were sent to stop them.

In March 1814 the HMS *Cherub* and HMS *Phoebe* battled the two American warships. HMS

During the battle against the HMS *Phoebe* and HMS *Cherub*, Midshipman Farragut kept a diary. This is what he wrote about his first big battle, "I performed the duties of captain's aid, **quarter-gunner, powder-boy,** and, in fact, did everything that was required of me. . . . When my services were not required for other purposes, I generally assisted in working a gun; would run and bring [gun]powder from the boys and send them back for more, until the captain wanted me to carry a message . . . "

means His Majesty's Ship and is an abbreviation used by the British navy for its ships, like the American navy uses USS. The battle lasted about two hours. The British ships had more cannons than the *Essex* and *Essex Junior.* Cannons from the British ships blasted away at the Americans, damaging their ships. Soon, Captain Porter surrendered his ships, and the fighting, the first large sea battle of Midshipman Farragut's career, ended.

The British captured the Americans and sent them home to the United States. Captain Porter was proud of his young midshipman and the excellent job he had done in battle. Farragut was also proud of his guardian, whom he cared for very much. James thought so highly of Captain Porter that after James returned home, he changed his first name to David, in honor of his guardian.

Shortly after David Farragut reached the United States, the War of 1812 ended. The United States had defeated Great Britain for the second time in 30 years. Now, the United States had strengthened its position in the world. Other countries respected the United States more than ever before.

After the war the navy gave David many other jobs. From 1815 to 1820, he served on warships in the Mediterranean Sea, where he learned the French, German, Spanish, and Arabic languages. In 1821 the navy promoted David to the rank of lieutenant. The next year, Lieutenant Farragut fought pirates in the West Indies.

After defeating these pirates, David returned to the United States in 1823 and moved to Norfolk,

Virginia, where he met and fell in love with Susan Marchant. They married in September 1823.

For the next 20 years, David had many other jobs in the navy. But in 1840, his wife died after a long illness. David missed his wife and he wanted to stay home in Norfolk, but the navy needed him. In 1841 the navy promoted him to the rank of commander. David's next major accomplishment for the navy was in helping to win the Mexican-American War.

In 1845 many nations including the United States considered Texas to be an independent country. Texas used to be part of Mexico. In 1836, Texas won a war of independence against this country. In 1845 the Mexican government considered Texas to still be part of Mexico.

Shortly after becoming U.S. president in 1845, James K. Polk asked the people of Texas to vote on whether or not they wanted to become part of the United States. This angered the Mexican people. Despite the Mexicans' anger, many Texans wanted to be Americans. On July 4,

The Battle of Palo Alto in May 1846, took place before President Polk signed a formal declaration of war with Mexico. The Mexican-American War would continue through 1847. At the end of the war, the Treaty of Guadalupe Hidalgo set the southern boundary of Texas and gave New Mexico and California to the United States.

1845, the people of Texas voted to become part of the United States.

American soldiers were sent to Texas in August 1845 to protect the newest part of their country. Over the next few months, the American and Mexican armies prepared for the possibility of war. In April 24, 1846, Mexican General Mariano Arista sent a letter to the U.S. Army, warning that he would fight the Americans unless they left Texas immediately. The next day, the Mexican army crossed the Rio Grande River, rode into Texas, and attacked. Sixteen American soldiers were killed or wounded in the battle, and the Mexican-American War began.

After the war, David returned to the United States where he helped build navy bases and was in charge of weapons and supplies in Norfolk, Virginia; Washington, D.C.; and Fort Monroe, Virginia. In 1855 the navy promoted him again, this time to the rank of captain.

In 1860 the United States found itself at the beginning of another war. This one would be a civil war that would break the country in half. Northern states would fight against Southern states. David's home was in Virginia, a Southern state that decided to fight against the Northern states of the country. Like many other Americans, Captain David Farragut had a choice to make–Should he fight for the North or help his Southern state (Virginia) fight against the North? This proved to be a very difficult decision for thousands of Americans.

Men, women, and children were taken from Africa and brought to the United States. They were then sold to plantation owners in the South. Slaves worked for little or no money in the fields and homes of their owners, and they had no rights or freedoms. This arrangement benefited the plantation owners and was an important part of the Southern economy. Plantation owners could operate their farms with very few expenses.

A Country Divided

In 1860 the United States was divided over the issue of slavery. Many people in the Northern states opposed slavery and wanted it to be abolished. Many Southerners supported slavery and did not want Northerners or the government in Washington, D.C., telling them whether or not they could own slaves. Wealthy Southerners bought African Americans and used them to do many things for them—cook, clean, farm, and work—for little or no money. These African Americans belonged to their owners and had no freedom.

As the United States grew, Northerners and Southerners argued about whether slavery should be

On February 8, 1861, representatives from seven Southern states agreed to create a new country, the Confederate States of America. These representatives also wrote laws for the Confederacy. One law said that slavery would be allowed everywhere in the Confederate States of America. The first seven Confederate states were Alabama, Florida, Georgia, Louisiana, Mississippi, South Carolina, and Texas. By the end of 1861, four more states seceded, or left the United States, and joined the Confederacy. These states were Arkansas, North Carolina, Tennessee, and Virginia.

permitted in the country's new states and territories. Northerners said no, but Southerners wanted slavery to be allowed everywhere. This argument had been going on for many years, without addressing what would happen to slavery.

In November 1860, Abraham Lincoln, from the Northern state of Illinois, was elected the 16th president of the United States. After Lincoln's election, most Southerners decided they did not want to be part of the United States anymore because the new president opposed slavery. One by one, beginning with South Carolina in 1860, the Southern states voted to secede from the

United States. This meant that they did not want to be part of the United States anymore and decided to form their own nation.

In July 1861 the Confederate States established their capital city in Richmond, Virginia. The United States, also called the **Union**, and the Confederate States were angry with each other, and America was on the verge of war. It was just a matter of time before someone fired the first shot.

On April 12, 1861, the Civil War began when Confederate soldiers fired on Fort Sumter, a fort held by the United States in the harbor of Charleston, South Carolina. After the fort surrendered, the **Confederacy** had its first victory of the war.

As the war began, David was almost 60 years old and living in Norfolk, Virginia, waiting for an assignment from the navy. On April 19, Virginia voted to secede from the United States and joined the Confederate States of America. Many

The first battle of the Civil War took place at Fort Sumter when Confederate soldiers attacked and had their first victory in the harbor of Charleston, South Carolina.

U.S. soldiers, officers, and sailors from Virginia decided to fight for their state. They left the Union army and joined the new Armed Forces of the Confederacy.

One of the most famous officers to leave the U.S. Army was the highly respected Colonel Robert E. Lee. President Lincoln thought so highly of him that he offered Lee the job of commander of the Union army. But Lee did not want to fight against his home state of Virginia where so many of his relatives lived. Lee was upset about the Civil War and the idea of battling other Americans. But he decided to fight for the new country, the Confederate States of America, against his old one. On April 20, Lee resigned from the U.S. Army.

David did not make the same choice as Lee. Like many other officers, he decided to stay loyal to the United States and fight against the **rebellious** Southern states. Since Virginia was now an enemy of the Union, David had to leave his home. He packed all his belongings and moved to Hastings-on-Hudson, which is a town just north of New York City in what is now Westchester County. After moving, David waited for the navy to give him a job to do.

At first the naval officials did not trust David. Many officers believed that David was loyal to

Virginia instead of the Union. They gave him many unimportant jobs until David convinced them he was devoted to the Union instead of the Confederacy. In December 1861, David received instructions to go to Washington. When he arrived there, Secretary of the Navy Gideon Welles gave David command of a **squadron** of U.S. navy ships that would go to the Gulf of Mexico. He ordered David to **blockade** the Southern ports on the gulf and capture the city of New Orleans, Louisiana. Secretary Welles picked David for such an important job because he had the best record of all U.S. senior naval officers available for the assignment. New Orleans was the Confederacy's largest city, and the sixth largest in both the Union and the Confederacy.

At the beginning of the Civil War, President Lincoln and General Winfield Scott, the general in chief of the Union army, decided to prevent the Confederacy from sending products to other countries by ship and receiving goods from them. The South did a lot of business with European countries. In exchange for tobacco and cotton, European nations sent many things to the Confederacy, such as machinery, clothing, and guns. Confederate leaders knew that to win the war, they needed to keep trading with Europe.

President Lincoln and Northern leaders also knew this. To prevent any ships from coming to or leaving Southern ports, the Union navy would have to blockade the Confederacy.

General Scott's plan for blockading Southern ports was called the Anaconda policy. It was named after the giant Anaconda snake, which wraps itself around its victims and then squeezes them to death. General Scott and President Lincoln wanted to do the same thing to the Confederacy–squeeze it to death by stopping any ships from entering or leaving Southern ports.

The Anaconda policy was a good plan. But nothing like it had ever been tried before. Many European leaders said it would be impossible for the plan to succeed.

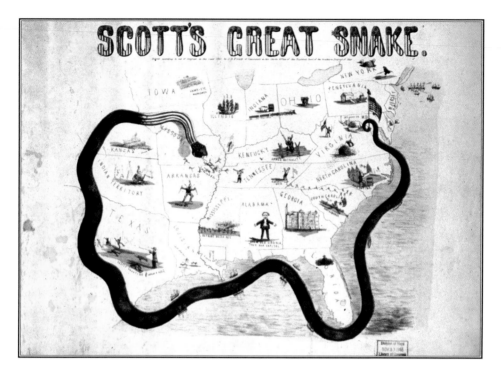

A map depicting General Winfield Scott's Anaconda plan. He wanted to have the Union navy block the Southern ports to stop any ships from bringing in supplies to the Confederacy.

David soon realized how hard it would be to blockade Southern ports. At the start of the war, the Union navy was very small. The Confederacy had at least 10 important ports, and 3,500 miles of coastline. There were not enough

Union ships to blockade all of this territory.

Early in the war, the Anaconda policy did not work very well. The Confederacy used small, fast ships called **blockade runners** to "outrun" the Union navy. Many of these blockade runners had engines that used coal or steam. These engines made them go faster than any Union ships, which only had sails for power. For every 1 blockade runner captured by the Union in 1861, at least 10 Confederate ships escaped.

There were many famous Confederate blockade runners. These ships escaped capture by the Union navy many times. One of the most famous was called the *Robert E. Lee*, named after the Confederate general. The ship mainly sailed in and out of Wilmington, North Carolina. The *Robert E. Lee* had a steam engine. Many sailors thought it was the fastest ship in either the Confederate States or the Union. The *Robert E. Lee* successfully ran the Union blockade an amazing 21 times, more than almost any other ship.

But slowly, the blockade began improving. The Union quickly built more ships, and added them to the Anaconda plan. The Secretary of the

The Confederacy used ships like this blockade runner to get past the Union navy and bring supplies and weapons to the Confederate army.

Navy also asked private ship owners to donate their vessels for use in the blockade.

Many more Confederate ships still escaped the blockade. David knew that the best way to stop this was to capture Southern ports, like New Orleans. Without ports, Southern ships and others wanting to dock at Confederate cities would have no place to go. On February 2, 1862, David and his squadron of 17 wooden ships left Hampton Roads, Virginia, a large port controlled by the Union. David was aboard a ship called the USS _Hartford_, which was powered by a steam engine. It took until February 20 for David's ships to steam from Virginia to the Gulf of Mexico and the mouth of the Mississippi River. This was where he began to plan the capture of New Orleans.

Union naval ships are shown here attacking the Confederate port of New Orleans.

3

The Hero of New Orleans

David's 17 ships were very powerful. They had a total of 154 cannons on board. David also had ships that carried very large guns called mortars, which shot much bigger shells than cannons could.

David planned to sail his ships up the Mississippi River to capture New Orleans. But the Confederates were ready for him. They had two forts, Fort St. Phillip and Fort Jackson, located on either side of the river. The forts had 157 cannons all pointed at ships on the Mississippi. There were also several Confederate warships waiting for the Union navy.

The USS *Monitor* and the CSS *Merrimack* fought in a battle of the ironclads on March 9, 1862, at Hampton Roads, Virginia. The battle lasted for hours because cannon balls just bounced off the metal plates on each ship.

Besides the cannons, forts, and ships, the Confederates had some surprises for David. They had tied a heavy chain across the river and put logs in the water to prevent ships from passing through.

As the Union ships moved up the river, David stopped before they reached the forts. The Confederates began firing their cannons, but the Union ships were too far away. The cannon balls could not reach them. But David was close enough to use his mortars. For six days, he bombarded the forts with hundreds of mortar shells. The Union ships shot so many mortar shells that they almost ran out of them. Despite this bombardment, David could not destroy the forts. His officers advised him to stop. The Union ships would not be able to reach land as long as the forts were not captured. Secretary Welles also told David to wait.

But David did not agree. He believed he had to attack before the Confederates became even stronger. David also knew that near New Orleans, the rebels were building a powerful **ironclad**, stronger than any of David's wooden ships. The commander wanted to attack

When the Civil War began, all ships were made of wood. In 1862 the Union and Confederate navies built two different kinds of ships. For the first time in history, **vessels** were covered with sheets of iron. These iron sheets would protect the ships from cannon balls so they could be almost unsinkable. These new ships were called ironclads. On March 9, 1862, the *Monitor*, a Union ironclad, and the *Merrimack*, a Confederate ironclad also called the *Virginia*, fought the first battle of ironclad ships. They battled for hours, and their cannon balls just bounced off the ships' metal plates.

before the Confederates finished building their ship, called the CSS (Confederate States Ship) *Louisiana*. David told his men to get ready to sail past the forts at night. He knew that the moon would not be very bright, and the Confederates would have trouble seeing the Union ships.

In the afternoon of April 23, David visited all 17 of his warships. He wanted to make sure his men understood their commander's orders. At 2 A.M., a signal of two red lights would be given from the *Hartford*, David's ship. That signal would mean start the attack.

After the signal was given, the Union fleet began moving. By about 3:30 in the morning, the Union ships reached the forts. Despite the darkness, the Confederates saw them, and one of the rebels fired a rocket into the sky to warn the other soldiers. The Confederate cannons began firing. David's ships returned fire. Suddenly, the dark night became bright.

The battle continued for almost two hours. David's ships cut through the chain across the river. They avoided the logs the Confederates tried to block them with. Many ships were damaged and some sank. Cannon balls and mortar shells from the Union ships heavily damaged the forts. By 5:30 A.M. the Confederates stopped firing their guns. Fourteen of David's ships passed the forts, and the Union navy had won the battle. The Confederates had sunk only three Union navy vessels. David had also destroyed the Confederate ships that waited for him next to the forts.

After the battle, David's ships stopped briefly so his men could repair some of the damage caused by enemy cannon fire. David also wanted his men to rest after their battle. Soon, his ships were moving again as they steamed up the Mississippi River toward New Orleans.

As the Union ships neared the city, Southerners knew David's fleet was coming, and they feared what would happen after the Union attacked. A Union army of about 15,000 soldiers, commanded by General Benjamin Butler, was also getting close to the city. On April 25,

David's fleet reached New Orleans. He sent a small boat with two officers to the shore. He ordered them to go into the city and tell the people there to surrender.

When these officers arrived, they went to city hall, the location of New Orleans' government. Angry mobs of people surrounded city hall and wanted to know who would protect them from the enemy invaders. These people also screamed at the two Union officers and some even pointed guns and threatened to shoot them. Finally, the officers entered the building and demanded that the city surrender. The mayor of New Orleans refused. Both sides argued for three days, but New Orleans would not surrender.

On April 28, David changed his strategy. He sent 250 marines and two cannons ashore. The marines marched up to city hall and pointed their guns at the building. Frightened by David's ships and marines, the mayor of New Orleans finally surrendered. He knew there was no Confederate army or navy nearby that was large

David Farragut's plan was to sail up the Mississippi River and capture Southern forts along the way. His ships are shown here passing the forts in April 1862.

enough to defeat David and General Butler. He had no choice but to give up.

David had won a great victory. His ships smashed the Confederate forts guarding the Mississippi River. These forts finally surrendered on April 28. The Union commander had captured the South's largest city without firing a shot. After hearing the news about the battle, Secretary

Welles was very happy with his commander. Southerners felt differently. They were sad and angry that the Union had captured New Orleans.

On May 1, General Butler and his army arrived in the city. New Orleans belonged to the Union again. With Butler's army now in control of the city, David took his ships up the Mississippi River. In June they steamed to Vicksburg, Mississippi. This city had a powerful fort, stronger than those guarding New Orleans, located on a hill high above the river. David tried blasting Vicksburg with cannon fire. But the city's fortifications were too high for David's cannons to reach them. In July, after patrolling up and down the Mississippi River, the Union naval commander ordered his ships to return to New Orleans. Before returning there, David's ships also captured two other Mississippi River cities, Baton Rouge, Louisiana, and Natchez, Mississippi.

On July 16, the U.S. Congress honored the man who was now being called the Hero of New Orleans. The Congress rewarded David for his victory by promoting him to the rank of rear **admiral.**

In August, David left New Orleans again and returned with his fleet to the Gulf of Mexico. There the Union ships would again **blockade** Southern ports. The ships first went to Pensacola, Florida. By the end of the year, David's fleet blockaded every Confederate port on the Gulf of Mexico, except for Mobile, Alabama. The Union now controlled almost the whole Gulf. While 1862 ended with lots of good news for the Union navy, the new year did not start out as well.

Confederate soldiers captured the port city of Galveston, Texas, in January 1863. They also sank four Union ships that David had sent to Galveston. While David focused on Galveston, a large, powerful Confederate ship called the CSS *Florida* escaped Union ships guarding Mobile Bay. David was embarrassed that the *Florida* got away from his ships.

In March, David and seven vessels returned to the Mississippi River. A Union army commanded by General Ulysses S. Grant planned to attack Vicksburg, Mississippi, on land. David used his

David's fleet played an important role in the combined land and sea siege of Vicksburg, Mississippi. Following the Union victory, David was allowed to return home to rest and visit with his family.

ships to keep Confederate forces south of the city from helping their army in Vicksburg. Another fleet, commanded by David Porter, plus Grant's army, all moved toward Vicksburg. On July 4, 1863, after a long **siege** by Grant's soldiers, the Confederates in Vicksburg surrendered to the

Union. Now the whole Mississippi River, from New Orleans north, was open to Union ships.

The Union's triumph at Vicksburg was very important. Around the same time, another Union army, commanded by General George Meade, defeated the Confederates at Gettysburg, Pennsylvania. These two victories hurt the South badly. Now, for probably the first time in the Civil War, many people started believing that the Union could win.

After the Vicksburg victory, David told another officer, "I am growing old fast, and need rest." Recognizing all he had done in fighting the Confederates, the navy decided this would be a good time for its most famous admiral to rest. Everyone knew much fighting still needed to be done to win the war. So on August 1, David steamed back to the Gulf of Mexico on board the *Hartford.* Following a nine-day voyage, the *Hartford* arrived in New York City. David now had time to rest and visit his family.

This drawing shows the Battle of Mobile Bay in Alabama.

"Damn the Torpedoes!"

David enjoyed his time in New York City. He visited with his family, which was close by in Hastings-on-Hudson. The people of New York welcomed the hero of New Orleans. Many people crowded around the *Hartford*, wanting to visit the admiral's ship and congratulate David for his many victories.

After spending the rest of the year in New York, David decided he was ready to leave. In early January 1864 he boarded the *Hartford* and sailed south. David headed back to the Gulf of Mexico where he planned to blockade Mobile, Alabama. This city was the only port on the gulf that the Confederacy still controlled. Blockade runners had been escaping the Union navy around Mobile Bay, the body of water outside the city of Mobile, for three and a half years.

David waited for about six months outside Mobile Bay for other warships and ironclads to join him. He also waited for Union soldiers to arrive so they could attack on land while David attacked by sea. While the soldiers and other warships traveled to David, he planned his strategy. He needed to learn about the Confederate defenses.

Two forts, Fort Morgan and Fort Gaines, guarded the entrance to Mobile Bay. The city of Mobile was at the northern end of the bay. The space between these two forts was only about three miles wide. This did not leave much room for ships to pass by, especially when they were under fire from the forts. The Confederates placed large logs and 180 torpedoes filled with explosives, also called mines, in the water to block enemy ships from entering the bay. A ship hitting one of them would blow up. There was only a narrow channel through the logs and minefield for blockade-runners and other friendly ships to pass through. Confederate ships knew the mines' locations, but David and the Union navy did not.

Besides the logs and mines, the Confederates also had four ships, including the ironclad *Tennessee*, waiting for the Union navy. For the last three and a half years, these four ships helped many blockade-runners escape the Union navy. David knew a lot about the enemy's defenses. Confederate **deserters** and people supporting the Union told him about the mines, logs, forts, and ships. But he still did not know exactly where the mines were in the water.

In early August, David had a fleet of 17 ships, including three ironclads ready to fight. On August 3, about 1,500 Union soldiers landed on the western end of Dauphin Island, which guarded the entrance to Mobile Bay. Fort Gaines

An example of a Union ironclad is shown here. David used ironclads and wooden ships in his assault on the forts in Mobile.

was located on the island's east end. The troops would attack the fort by land, while the Union navy tried sailing past the fort and up the bay.

The next day, David met with his officers to discuss strategy for the battle. The Union iron-clads would steam in front of the 14 wooden ships and clear a path through the minefield. David knew that cannonballs from the Confederate forts would just bounce off the ironclads. The wooden ships would be tied together to help each other stay afloat if gunfire damaged any of them.

David told his officers to put sand bags and covers on the ships' decks and around the machinery. This should help prevent any fires from starting if rebel cannon balls struck the ships. By sunset, the USS *Tecumseh*, a new ironclad, arrived and joined David's fleet. The 18 Union ships and soldiers waited for David's order to attack.

While the Union forces prepared for battle, so did the Confederates. In Fort Gaines and Fort Morgan, soldiers gathered as many cannon balls as they could find. Colonel Charles Anderson commanded Fort Gaines, the larger of the two bases. By the end of the day on August 4, he had about 800 Confederate soldiers in the fort. He was ordered to prevent the Union from capturing Fort Gaines no matter what.

At about 3 A.M. on August 5, David ordered his fleet to begin moving. Sailors had prepared the cannons for firing. The wooden ships were tied together. David decided to tie himself to the top of one of the *Hartford's* masts. Masts are long wooden posts that contain sails and ropes. He wanted to be able to see what was happening in the battle. Being so high up, he thought, he could see over any smoke or fire caused by cannon fire.

By about 6 A.M., the USS *Brooklyn,* one of David's ships, was the first to move toward Mobile Bay. The men aboard the other 17 ships cheered as they followed the *Brooklyn's* path.

Around 6:30, David's fleet approached Fort Morgan, the closest of the two Confederate forts to the bay's entrance. The *Tecumseh* fired its guns at the fort, and the Battle of Mobile Bay began. The Union ships moved past the fort, firing all their cannons at the enemy. The troops in Fort Morgan fired back. Before the battle, the Confederates had put their cannonballs into the fort's furnaces to make them red-hot. When these hot cannon balls hit David's wooden ships,

David was perched on his ship's mast when he shouted down to his men, "Damn the torpedoes. Full steam ahead!" He inspired the sailors to continue their fight to victory.

they tore large holes in them. Fires spread across several Union vessels, including the *Hartford.*

While the wooden ships battled Fort Morgan, the *Tecumseh* moved through the minefield. As the *Tecumseh* steamed through the mines, it turned to attack the Confederate ironclad

Tennessee. As the Union ship turned, there was a tremendous explosion. The loud noise seemed to stop the battle for a moment as everyone looked to see what had happened. The *Tecumseh* had struck a mine and quickly sank, killing all the men on board.

The rest of the fleet's sailors and officers were upset about the *Tecumseh.* They seemed not to know what to do next. The *Brooklyn* stopped moving almost completely. Seeing that their enemy was confused, Fort Morgan's gunners fired even more cannon balls at the Union ships. David knew that his men were in trouble and that he had to do something to help them. High on the *Hartford's* mast, David screamed down to the pilot, the sailor driving the *Hartford,* "Damn the torpedoes. Full speed ahead!" These famous words inspired the sailors and officers to keep fighting.

The *Hartford* quickly picked up speed and turned to the left, trying to get through the mine-field. Soon, David's ship made it safely through the mines and moved out of range of Fort Morgan's guns. The four Confederate ships, including the *Tennessee*, quickly moved in to attack. But the crew of the *Hartford* was ready for them. They fired at the three smallest Confederate ships and quickly either sank or damaged them. Only one Confederate ship, the *Tennessee*, was left.

By this time, the rest of David's fleet had moved safely through the minefield. The USS *Hartford* led six other ships to attack the CSS *Tennessee*. The *Tennessee* was badly outnumbered, but its crew fought bravely.

The *Tennessee* tried ramming the wooden Union ships to sink them, and fired its cannons from as close as three feet away. David's ships fired their cannons back at point blank range. Soon, the *Tennessee* was badly damaged. It moved slowly away from the Union ships. Admiral Franklin Buchanan, commander of the Confederate fleet, was on board the *Tennessee*. When told about the damage to the ironclad, he

An officer leans against a large mortar, the most powerful guns used in the Civil War.

said, "Do the best you can, and when all is done, surrender."

At 10 A.M., the *Tennessee* could not fight anymore. The ship's captain, James Johnston, raised a white flag to surrender. When David's men saw the white flag, they stopped firing at the *Tennessee* and cheered the ironclad's surrender.

Later that day, David congratulated his men for their victory over the Confederate forces and wrote a letter to them praising them for their courage. He also admitted how worried he had been about the Confederate minefield. David wrote that he feared that Union ships might have hit mines and exploded as soon as they entered the bay.

David now moved toward Fort Gaines. His ships fired their cannons at the Confederate positions. While Union ships attacked from the sea, about 3,000 Union soldiers attacked on land. David moved his ironclads as close to the fort as possible and ordered them to fire. The 100-pound shells from the Union ships' guns badly damaged the fort. But the Confederates' 32-pound shells just bounced off the ironclads' armor. The soldiers inside the fort fought as hard as they could. Some of these troops were only 13, 14, and 15 years old and students at a Southern military school. They were fighting in their first battle. By the end of the day on August 6, all of Fort

Both sides used many different guns during the Civil War. One of the most famous was a mortar called "The Dictator." This Union gun was so big that only a specially built railroad car could move it. The Dictator weighed over 17,000 pounds. It could hurl cannonballs farther than almost any other gun in the war. This huge mortar could shoot 200 pound cannonballs and hit targets about two and a half miles away. Mortars were valuable to both sides. They were the biggest and most powerful guns used in the Civil War.

Gaines's cannons, except one, had been destroyed. There was almost nothing left to shoot with.

On August 7, David sent a small boat with a white flag from the *Hartford* toward the fort. When the boat arrived at Fort Gaines, the Union sailors demanded the Confederates give up. Several Confederate officers rowed back to the *Hartford* with the Union sailors. Once on board, David served them wine and told them they had no hope of winning. The Confederates, including fort commander Colonel Anderson, looked around at all the Union ships waiting to begin firing again.

Once back inside the fort, Anderson decided his men had no chance against the Union navy. On August 8, Fort Gaines surrendered. But there was still fighting at Fort Morgan. Union soldiers had laid siege to the fort and prevented any help from reaching the rebels inside. David's ships and Union cannons on land fired at the fort and it was badly damaged. After about two weeks, Fort Morgan finally gave up. The Battle of Mobile Bay was over.

The Union navy now controlled the entrance to all Confederate ports in the Gulf of Mexico. Although the city of Mobile did not surrender to the Union until April 1865, David's fleet could prevent any ships from entering or leaving Mobile Bay. The city was cut off by sea from the rest of the world.

David's victory at Mobile Bay was very important. Before the battle, the Union had not won a fight against the Confederates for about nine months. Many in the North had begun worrying that the war might never end. Even David at one time worried about the war. Before the battle, he wrote, "I am *depressed* by the bad news from every direction. The enemy seem to be . . . whipping us in every direction. . . . *I get right sick,* every now and then, at the bad news."

But David's success at Mobile Bay changed that feeling. **Morale** in the Union states rose. People felt optimistic about defeating the Confederacy. David Farragut was even a bigger hero now than after the Battle of New Orleans. He had become one of the country's most famous men.

David was exhausted after the battle. Many of his officers noticed how tired he looked. In September, he wrote a letter to Secretary of the Navy Welles. David said, "I fear . . . my health is giving way. . . . [T]he last six months have been a severe drag upon me, and I want rest . . ." But the war still had several months left to go, and the navy had other assignments for its most famous admiral.

Admiral David Farragut was sent to North Carolina in 1864 to continue the fight against Confederate block runners.

War Hero

Although David wanted to rest, the navy needed the Hero of Mobile Bay and New Orleans. The navy sent him to North Carolina to attack Confederate Fort Fisher, located near Wilmington. This was the only Confederate port still open to blockade runners.

The navy decided the port must be closed. This was important to winning the war. At this time in late 1864, Union troops commanded by General William Tecumseh Sherman were marching north through Georgia and South Carolina. The navy wanted to capture Wilmington and prevent the rebels from bringing supplies into the North Carolina port that could be used to stop Sherman. Secretary Welles ordered David to command the attack because David was the best rear admiral in the navy.

But Secretary Welles and the navy did not know the extent of David's exhaustion. Many of the officers and sailors who spent time with him after the Battle of Mobile Bay noticed that their commander looked sick. The 63-year-old needed rest, and he asked the navy not to send him to North Carolina. David's request was granted, and he did not have to go to North Carolina. Instead, he went to New York and was told to rest. He steamed north to New York aboard the *Hartford.*

When his ship entered New York harbor, a small boat filled with many New York City government leaders and important citizens wanted to greet David right away. When they climbed aboard the *Hartford* and met David they told him how much they, New York City, and the whole country appreciated his victory at Mobile Bay. David was touched by their kind words. He thanked them and prepared the *Hartford* for its docking in New York.

When his ship docked, many people crowded around. They shouted David's name and wanted him to know how proud they were of him. That night, David went to a party in New York City where even more people came to thank him for defeating the Confederates. Even strangers wanted to shake the hand of the war hero.

David spent several more days in New York. He told people about his many victories over the Confederates, especially the one at Mobile Bay. New Yorkers wanted to give David a gift, thanking him for all he did for the country. They invited him to live in New York and New York City's leaders gave him $50,000 toward the purchase of a house. This was an enormous amount of money in 1864, worth several times more than it is today. David graciously accepted the generous gift. He also said that he would be honored to live in New York. There would be more honors for this hero. On December 23, 1864, President Lincoln promoted David to the rank of vice admiral.

David spent the Christmas and New Year's holidays in New York. He was feeling much better than he had before coming here from Mobile Bay. David enjoyed his new home and looked forward to spending more time there.

In late January 1865 the navy decided it needed Vice Admiral Farragut again. At that time, several Confederate warships were attacking Union soldiers and destroying supplies in Virginia. The navy wanted David to stop the Confederates and sink their ships. David went to Virginia, ready to fight again. But by the time he arrived there, Union ships and soldiers had already defeated the enemy. David was not needed after all. Instead of returning to New York, David went to Washington, D.C.

In April 1865, Union troops surrounded Richmond and the Army of Northern Virginia,

Confederate General Robert E. Lee was a skilled military leader in the U.S. Army before the Civil War began and he decided to fight for the South. After Lee retreated from Virginia, Union soldiers marched into the Confederate capital.

commanded by General Robert E. Lee. During the night of April 2, Lee took his troops out of Richmond and retreated from the Union soldiers. Lee's troops needed food, water, and equipment. They could not fight the larger and stronger Union army. Instead, Lee and his men retreated west, where they hoped to join other Confederate troops and then return to fight the Union.

After Lee's troops left Richmond, Union soldiers entered the Confederate capital. David went with them. He wanted to return to his home state of Virginia. After spending a few days in Richmond, he traveled to Norfolk. He visited his old house and also met many old friends. But they were not happy to see David. They were angry with him for fighting with the Union, against his state, his friends, and his neighbors. David tried to explain his decision. He told them he could not fight against the United States. But they remained very angry with him. David could not change their minds and they could not change his about the war. When he left Norfolk several days later, he never went back.

Robert E. Lee surrendered the Army of Northern Virginia to General Ulysses S. Grant at Appomattox Court House, Virginia, ending the Civil War.

On April 9, 1865, Confederate General Robert E. Lee surrendered his army to Union General Ulysses S. Grant. The Civil War had ended. Americans almost could not believe the war was finally over. Many changes had happened in the five years since the war began. More than 610,000 soldiers and sailors from both sides had been killed during the conflict between the North and South. Over 500,000 soldiers and sailors had been wounded. Slaves in the Southern states were now all free. Large parts of the South, especially in David's old home state of Virginia, had been destroyed by the war. Trees had been destroyed by the armies during the fighting. Thousands of farm animals were dead. Many cities had been ruined.

Now that all the battles were over, the North and South could unite again. People began putting the country back together. But on April 15, Americans were shocked and saddened to learn that President Lincoln had been assassinated. He was shot while watching a play with his wife at Ford's Theater in Washington, D.C. John Wilkes Booth, who supported the Confederacy, killed Lincoln because he was angry the Union had won the war.

After the war, David stayed in the navy. During the summer of 1865, David traveled to New England. On his trip, many people thanked him for helping to defeat the Confederacy. David was treated like a hero and honored for his many victories. On July 26, 1866, Congress created the rank of full admiral just for David. He became the only admiral in the entire United Stated Navy.

In 1867 the navy appointed him commander of the European Squadron, a group of warships assigned to travel to many European countries. David and his officers and sailors would be goodwill ambassadors for the United States, making friends in Europe. On June 28, 1867, his squadron left New York.

For the next 17 months, David's ships traveled to many European countries—Belgium,

On September 30, 1870, David Farragut was buried in New York City. Many people came to honor the great hero of the Civil War. Ulysses S. Grant, then the president of the United States, came to his funeral. So did the president's advisers, the governor of New York, New York City Mayor James Wilson, and Union General George Meade, who won the Battle of Gettysburg during the Civil War. There were also more than 10,000 soldiers, all there to honor the great war hero.

Denmark, England, France, Greece, Holland, Italy, Russia, Spain, and Sweden. David was greeted as a hero everywhere he went.

He returned to the United States in 1869 and traveled to California during the summer. While traveling across the country from California to New York, David had a heart attack during a stop in Chicago, Illinois. David never fully recovered. He traveled to Portsmouth, New Hampshire, where the navy had a large base.

On August 10, 1870, David Farragut died in Portsmouth. He was 69 years old. David's many Civil War victories helped the Union defeat the Confederate States of America. He would be remembered as one of America's greatest naval war heroes.

GLOSSARY

admiral–highest ranking officer in the navy.

blockade–to prevent someone or something from entering or leaving a place.

blockade runners–Confederate ships that tried to escape from the Union blockade of Southern cities during the Civil War.

Confederacy–another name for the Southern states during the Civil War.

deserters-soldiers who run away from their army during a war.

ironclad–an iron or metal covered warship invented during the Civil War.

morale–the emotional state of an individual or group.

quarter-gunner–a sailor on a warship who helps fire the cannons.

powder-boy–a young sailor who carries gunpowder to cannons on a warship.

rebellion–a violent revolt against a government.

rebellious–people who participate in a violent revolt against a country.

siege–when an army surrounds an enemy town or city.

squadron–a group of warships.

Union–another name for the Northern states during the Civil War.

vessel–another word for ship.

CHRONOLOGY

1801   Born James Glasgow Farragut on July 5 in Campbell's Station, Tennessee.

1810   Enters the U.S. Navy as a midshipman.

1813   Becomes commander of the USS *Essex Junior* and fights Great Britain in the War of 1812.

1814   Changes his first name to David, in honor of his guardian, David Porter.

1821   Promoted to lieutenant in the navy.

1823   Moves to Norfolk, Virginia, and marries Susan Marchant in September.

1841   Becomes a commander in the U.S. Navy.

1845   Goes to Mexico to fight in the Mexican-American War.

1855   Becomes a captain in the navy.

1861   Decides to fight for the North in the Civil War and moves from Virginia to New York.

1862   Captures New Orleans, Louisiana, and is promoted to rear admiral.

1863   Helps capture Vicksburg, Mississippi.

1864   Defeats the Confederates at the Battle of Mobile Bay and is promoted to vice admiral.

1865   Returns to Virginia; the Civil War ends.

1866   Becomes an admiral in the navy.

1867   Travels to Europe as Commander of the U.S. Navy's European Squadron.

1870   Dies on August 10, 1870, in Portsmouth, New Hampshire.

CIVIL WAR TIME LINE ═══════════

1860   Abraham Lincoln is elected president of the United States on November 6. During the next few months, Southern states begin to break away from the Union.

1861   On April 12, the Confederates attack Fort Sumter, South Carolina, and the Civil War begins. Union forces are defeated in Virginia at the First Battle of Bull Run (First Manassas) on July 21 and withdraw to Washington, D.C.

1862   Robert E. Lee is placed in command of the main Confederate army in Virginia in June. Lee defeats the Army of the Potomac at the Second Battle of Bull Run (Second Manassas) in Virginia on August 29–30. On September 17, Union general George B. McClellan turns back Lee's first invasion of the North at Antietam Creek near Sharpsburg, Maryland. It is the bloodiest day of the war.

1863   On January 1, President Lincoln issues the Emancipation Proclamation, freeing slaves in Southern states. Between May 1–6, Lee wins an important victory at Chancellorsville, but key Southern commander Thomas J. "Stonewall" Jackson dies from wounds. In June, Union forces hold the city of Vicksburg, Mississippi, under siege. The people of Vicksburg surrender on July 4. Lee's second invasion of the North during July 1–3 is decisively turned back at Gettysburg, Pennsylvania.

1864   General Grant is made supreme Union commander on March 9. Following a series of costly battles, on June 19 Grant successfully encircles Lee's troops in Petersburg, Virginia. A siege of the town lasts nearly a year. Union general William Sherman captures Atlanta on September 2 and begins the "March to the Sea," a campaign of destruction across Georgia and South Carolina. On November 8, Abraham Lincoln wins reelection as president.

1865   On April 2, Petersburg, Virginia, falls to the Union. Lee attempts to reach Confederate forces in North Carolina but is gradually surrounded by Union troops. Lee surrenders to Grant on April 9 at Appomattox, Virginia, ending the war. Abraham Lincoln is assassinated by John Wilkes Booth on April 14.

FURTHER READING

Beller, Susan Provost. *Never Were Men so Brave—The Irish Brigade During the Civil War.* New York: Simon & Schuster, 1998.

Clayton, Nancy. *Strange but True Civil War Stories.* Lowell, Mass.: Lowell House, 1999.

Grabowski, Patricia A. *Robert E. Lee—Confederate General.* Philadelphia: Chelsea House Publishers, 2001.

Herbert, Janis. *The Civil War for Kids—A History with 21 Activities.* Chicago: Chicago Review Press, 1999.

Lester, Julius. *From Slave Ship to Freedom Road.* New York: Dial Books, 1998.

PICTURE CREDITS

INDEX

Note: **Boldface** numbers indicate illustrations.

abolition of slavery, 23–24
admiral, 42, 71
Alexander Barclay, 15
American Revolution, 11
Anaconda policy, 29–33, **30**
Anderson, Charles, 51 , 58–59
Appomattox Courthouse, 69, **69**
Arista, Mariano, 20
Army of Northern Virginia, 66
assassination of Lincoln, 70

Baton Rouge, Louisiana, 42
blockade, 28–33, **30**, 43
blockade runners, 31–33, **32**, 48, 49
Booth, John Wilkes, 70
Brooklyn, 52, 54
Buchanan, Franklin, 55
Butler, Benjamin, 39–40, 42

California, 19
Campbell's Station, Tennessee, 7
cannons, 35
Cape Horn, 12, 14
Charleston, South Carolina, 26
Cherub, 15
Chesapeake, 11
Chicago, Illinois, 72
Chile, 14
Civil War, 7, 20–21, 23–34
Confederacy, 25
Confederate States of America, 24–25
cotton fields, **22**
CSS (Confederate States Ship), 38

Dauphin Island, 49
death of Farragut, 72
deserters, 49
"Dictator, The," 58

Essex Junior, 14–16
Essex, 10–16, **14**
European Squadron, 71–72

Farragut, David, **62**
Farragut, Elizabeth, 7–8
Farragut, George, 7, 10
ferryboats, 8
Florida, 43
Ford's Theater, 70
Fort Fisher, 63
Fort Gaines, 48–62
Fort Jackson, 35
Fort Monroe, Virginia, 20
Fort Morgan, 48–62
Fort St. Phillip, 35
Fort Sumter, 25, **26**

Galveston, Texas, 43
Georgia, 63
Gettysburg, Pennsylvania, 45, 71
Grant, Ulysses S., 43–44, 69, **69**, 71
Great Britain, 7, 11–12, 14, 17
Guadalupe Hidalgo, Treaty of, 19
Gulf of Mexico, 28, 33, 43–47, 59

Hamilton, Paul, 10
Hampton Roads, Virginia, 33, 36
Hartford, 33, 38, 45, 47, 52–58, 64–65
Hastings-on-Hudson, New York, 27, 47
Hero of New Orleans, 42
HMS (His Majesty's Ship), 15–16

ironclads, 37–38, 49, **50**, 51, 53–56

Johnston, James, 56

Lee, Robert E., 26–27, 67–68, **67**, 69, **69**
Lieutenant Farragut, 17

Lincoln, Abraham, 24, 26–29, 66, 70
Louisiana, 38

Macedonian, **6**
Marchant, Susan, 18
Meade, George, 45, 71
Merrimack, 36, 37
Mexican–American War, 18–20
Mexico, 18–20
midshipman, 10
mines, 48–49
Mississippi River, 33–43, **41**
Mobile, Alabama, 43, 47–64, **46**
Monitor, 36, **36**, 37
Monroe, James, 11
morale, 60
mortars, 35, **56**, 58

Natchez, Mississippi, 42
New Hampshire, 13
New Mexico, 19
New Orleans, Louisiana, 8–9, 28,
    33–35, **34**, 39, 43, 60–63
New York City, 64–66, 71
Norfolk, Virginia, 17–18, 20, 25, 68

Palo Alto, Battle of, **19**
Pensacola, Florida, 43
Phoebe, 15
Polk, James K., 18
Porter, David, 8–9, **9**, 15–17, 44
Portsmouth, New Hampshire, 72
powder boy, U.S. Navy, **13**, 16

quarter gunner, 16

rear admiral, 42
rebels, 27
Richmond, Virginia, 66, 68
Rio Grande River, 20
Robert E. Lee, 31

Scott, Winfield, 28–29
secession, 24
Secretary of the Navy, 10
Sherman, William Tecumseh, 63
siege of Vicksburg, 44–45
slavery, **22**, 23–24, 70
South Carolina, 24, 63
Spain, 14
squadron, 28
surrender of Lee, 69, **69**

Tecumseh, 51–53
Tennessee, 49, 54–56
Texas, 18–20
torpedoes, 48–49
Treaty of Guadalupe Hidalgo, 19

Union, 25
United States Navy, 6, 10
United States, **6**
USS (United States Ship), 10

Valparaiso, Chile, 14
vessels, 15
vice admiral, 66
Vicksburg, Mississippi, 42, 43–45, **44**
Virginia, 66
Virginia, 37

War of 1812, 6, 7, 11–12, 17
warships, 10
Washington, D.C., 20, 66
Welles, 42, 60, 64
West Indies, 17
Wilmington, 63
Wilson, James, 71

yellow fever, 8

ABOUT THE AUTHOR

BRUCE ADELSON has written 12 books for adults and children, including *Brushing Back Jim Crow—The Integration of Minor League Baseball in the American South* and *The Composite Guide to Field Hockey,* as well as three other historical biographies for children. A former elementary school substitute teacher and former commentator for National Public Radio and CBS Radio, Bruce is currently a book/multimedia reviewer for Children's Literature, a practicing attorney, and the proud father of Michael Daniel who was born in April 2001.